Articulation

of the Physical, Mental, and Spiritual

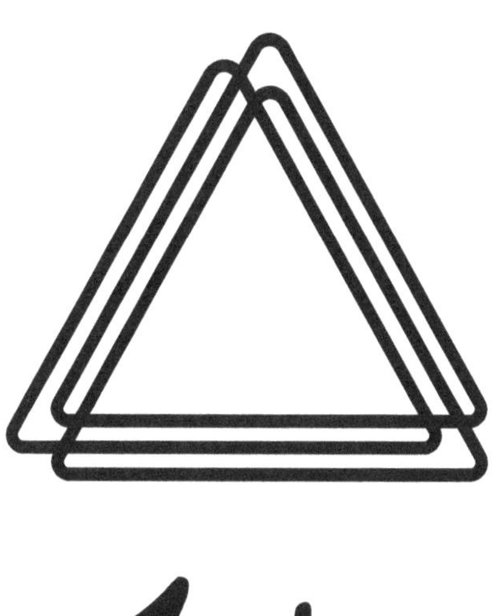

Zachx

Art and Design by Zachx

ISBN: 979-8-218-13180-7

DEDICATION:

This book is dedicated to my Lord and Savior, Jesus Christ. Without Him, I would not be able to achieve any of my goals or create any of the art that I have created. I also would like to dedicate this book to my love for the everlasting support, inspiration, and love that I am given. A final dedication to my family and friends for the support and love that has been projected towards me. I am grateful, elated, and a bit nervous to be sharing this project.

DISCLAIMER:

The opinions and beliefs expressed in this body of work are of the author's perspective and are not necessarily law. Please respect this as we are all entitled to our own opinions and beliefs.

The Artist's Duty

I believe that if somebody is gifted with a talent for art of sorts,
It is their absolute duty to share it with the world.

Core Belief

The core belief that I possess is that in this life,
Literally anything is possible because Jesus Christ exists.

Brokenheartedness

Human to breathe, drink, and bleed
Similar fluids—same needs.
When the body's heart and brain
Are confused and interchanged
Within, the mind and the soul,
Drowned in emotions, are woe.
Physical love is hatred
When spiritual life's death.

The Arts

There exists ideas that are so multi-faceted–that are Creation's heart.
Certain aspects of it are too idolized while others fade in the dark.
Humanity would not advance in skill, science, or medicine without art.
It possesses the ability to transform negative ideations into a healing fresh start.

Amethyst Mystique

Your intellect is a deep shade,
And your bones are sturdy.
You may be overlooked by many,
But those who don't take the time
To appreciate an inspiring shape,
Don't deserve its offerings–unworthy.
You are so vibrant unlike any
Other; I'm in awe of your mind.
Your skull is a winding cave
Filled with darkness and worries,
But beyond those, it is plenty.
Your mind is a mine; I crave you as mine.
Your thoughts can be dangerous to wade,
But within them, I unearthed beauty.
Explosives or treasures–my discovery.
Digging through the dark, I see what shines.

Skin

Your flesh is soft.
I must be gentle.
I tend to cause rot,
But it is all mental.
I am bruised by thought–
Healing isn't so simple.
I must remember. I ought
To realize that symbols
And coverings are not
The only aspect or whole.

Keys, Wallet, Phone

I brought my keys, wallet, and phone,
But I left my heart back at home.
The basic "necessities" that rule our lives
Don't even breathe or think and aren't alive.
With these, we can go home or travel away.
If we forget one, our peace is at stake.
Why do we rely so much on these things?
Why can't we relax and without them think?

Wanderer

I sit–I wonder;
That's how I wander.
My warm body remains
As my soul breaks chains.
I've traversed further, though
My flesh hasn't broken its pose.
My mind is a shuttle that takes me
Far away and drowns me in the deep.

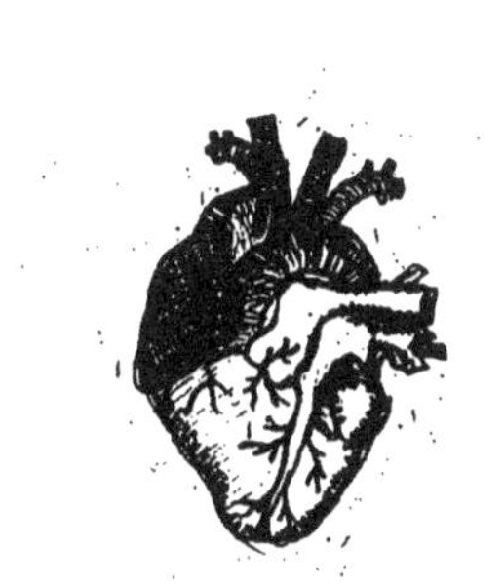

Sleep Habits

I should be asleep.
Though I am in bed,
I stay awake and think.
I'll be tired when I awaken.

Addictive

Addictions are addictive.
They go nameless.
I refuse to admit it.
It's difficult to evict them.
Addictions claim residency
In my time and in my mind.
When there is a vacancy
In aspects of my life.
Addictions take control.
These decisions are cold.
Despising myself to the soul
After they fill their mold.
Addictions feel good initially,
But that feeling is fleeting.
It is desolate and empty.
Numbness inhibits guilty feelings.

Diamondheart

Your heart, mind, and soul are as opal—mesmerizing.
You want armor for your finger; a metal band.
It's ironic that my birthstone is the common ring.
I want to meet the desires of your left hand;
Is it pride that causes my heart's hardening?
I cannot explain it, and nobody understands.
I suppose given my nature, this stone is fitting.
I just wince at the idea of meeting societal demands.

I hurt you...

I hurt you,
And I don't know why.
I hurt you.
It wasn't the first time.
I hurt you.
I saw you begin to cry.
I hurt you.
There was more than tears in your eyes.
I hurt you.
That low felt so high.
I hurt you
Because of my sick mind.
I hurt you,
And now I want to die.
I hurt you
Over a lack of compromise.
I hurt you.
Numbness leads to demise.
I hurt you.
Carelessness creates a painful divide.
I hurt you
Because of emotions I fight.
I hurt you.
That wrong felt so right.
I hurt you.
Empathy of the aftermath leads the wise.
I hurt you.
For all of this, I apologize.

Finding Rainbows

It amazes me that you can find
Rainbows in any situation.
People are often so blind
To the colors that face them,
But you can always seem to find
Rainbows though your clouds
Are heavily saturated in your mind.
They are filled with sorrow and doubt,
Yet you still seek rainbows to find.
Your rainbows are sought in any murky place.
Not only in beauty, you take the time
To carefully inspect it all just in case.
These are not always so hard to find.
You create rainbows to appreciate.
Colors that are hiding in plain sight
Awaiting somebody like you to illustrate.

Unfriended

You'll probably never read this,
But in the slight chance if you do–
You won't know that it's about you.
I'm sure you don't even consider
The fact that I think about these things
From time to time–in my head it rings.
It's likely nothing to you because you
Have your own life apart from mine.
You probably don't spend any time
Thinking about how excommunication
Often affects my emotional state.
You removed me from your slate
Without explaining the reason behind it.
Did I do something that offended?
Maybe you should've reprimanded.
I'm sorry if there's a wronging against you.
I still don't know what I've done
To make you feel that you need to shun.
I won't ever ask, and I'll always wonder,
But that doesn't mean that I don't
Want to know why though I won't.
I just crave deep connections with people,
But nobody wants to spend the energy
Or time creating a bond with synergy.
So, I'll sit alone at night and feel sorrow
And regret for all of the possibilities
Of the reason while succumbing to anxieties.
I'll accept it, but I will often reflect on this.

Alcohol Based

Why are people so obsessed with alcohol?
I'm either not drinking enough or not drinking at all.
Why do you care so much about my intake?
You're the one making all of these mistakes
With an excessive amount in your system.
I have a point, but nobody wants to listen.
Too much of anything can be dangerous.
Given my family history, I'm especially cautious.
I'm not sorry for my decisions to be frugal
With what causes people to be delusional.
If the cost of intelligent choices is to be mocked,
Then bring on the judgment and the scoffs.
I'll handle my drinks, and you handle what's in your hand.
This concept creates anxiety in which people are ignorant.
We all exist in such an alcohol based society,
And this is my sanitizer to help with my sanity.

Godforsaken

There is no point in trying to mask these thoughts.
You know what I think and feel, though I've fought
To ensure that I never cross that line of disrespect.
Why am I lying to myself and attempting to You?
That is completely senseless because You know.
You are aware without the confessions I disclose.
I am simply being honest in this time that I reflect.
Why is there prayer if Your Will is what You'll do?
Or are You waiting on the perfect timing of it all
Before You make judgment calls and humanity falls?
I needed help, and I sought in ways I never imagined.
I thought I was on the right track to bring healing.
Never before had I felt the strength and confidence,
But as it turned out, false hope kept me in suspense.
I'm aware, and I'll admit that I lack in our relationship–
I just thought that pleading in pain and trust would bring
The results that would protect me from immense hurt.
Why was I expecting what I know I don't deserve?
What I didn't initially take care of, how can I even mend?
Where do I even begin? I have ideas, but I'm unsure.
I still feel the ache and suffer almost every night.
I don't like to sleep at night because of sorrow I fight.
Such grief runs so deep, and I want it cleansed.
I ask for things here and there, and I feel ignored.
Though, it's true, I don't uphold my end of it.
Sometimes, I question if I even want all of this.
I feel so stupid when I partake in these traditions.
I hate that; I just want to celebrate it in the way
That my peers seem to be capable–I feel pathetic.
I feel numb to You, and regrettably, I'm apathetic.
I know that is wrong of me, but it's subconscious.
My conscious mind knows to fight that and pray.
Please, I plead that You forgive me of my sins.
I just don't know how to crave that desire again.
My heart is deceitful, yet I keep knowingly listening.
I know I am saved by grace through faith, and I trust.
There are moments where You remind me why;
I just wish that I wasn't so hardened and blind.
I keep waiting until I'm ready, but that is unwise of me.
To myself, cease being stubborn and selfish–polish the rust.

Aftermath

After spending all day trying to socially perform,
My genuineness seems to be deformed.
With each passing moment, I have to meet criteria
That is the standard of my age group.
Of all of my kind, trying to fit in, I am a letter
Attempting to blend with a group of numbers.
The aftermath of this isn't quite algebra.
There is no answer—my thoughts feud.
After what feels like failing to add to the crowd,
I am alone with thoughts that are silently loud.
I want to subtract all the negative confusion I face;
I just don't fit the shapes of the options available.
I feel internally divided with no room for positivity
Because I'll never solve the equation of humanity.
My emotions multiply, creating mixed feelings of fate.
I just don't know how to be normal while sitting at the adult tables.

You are a work of art.

People say you're a piece of work.
I say you're a work of art—great worth.
You think you're an embarrassment,
But I think you're an accomplishment.

Coming Chapters

I just don't know what I want presently
Other than you—that much I do know.
I just cannot justify mirroring your desires
Simply to bring you contentment and relief.
I hate myself for having such complexities,
And what I want least is to hurt your soul.
I must be totally candid with you, not a liar,
Or of your time and love, neither a thief.
I'm sure we'll align in time—I have a feeling.
My mind cannot fathom dreams you hold.
I'll understand if you go—decisions are dire.
I'll love you regardless of fate or other beliefs.

Bruised / Black & Blue

There is much injustice in such a cruel world.
The answer is not destruction, division, and chaos,
But it is actually construction, unity, and peace.
Racism and murder combatting racism and murder
Doesn't achieve the outcome that is sought.
Riots aren't displaying the strong, but the weak.
Protesting is requited because order is out-of-order.
Brutality is undeniable, and it should be fought.
You're wrong–to those who simply deny and disagree.
Now is not the time to be dated and stubborn.
It is the time to realize people are distraught
For a sensible reason, and we all need healing.
Stop justifying the double-sided evilness on Earth.
Humble yourselves and kill your prejudiced thoughts.
Imagine your mind, heart, and soul in another's body.
Don't just put away your hatred and pride, let it burn
Instead of victimizing the cities to fire and rot.
We share similar blood, so we should be family.
Humanity has contusions that continue to hurt unheard.
Left untreated, what comorbidities could it cause?
Treat lives with kindness and respect, and treat
The symptoms that grow deep in our dirt.
Think deeper and imagine their pain and the cost.
It's easy to write off and start ignorantly ignoring.
Everybody has specific struggles they stand under;
When you don't understand, don't discredit and mock.
Meet people where they're at while loving and supporting.

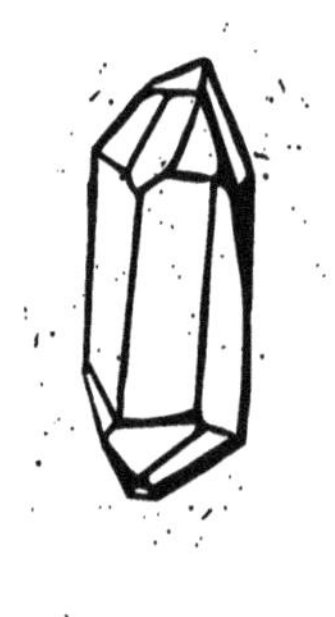

Josh

A name that is not my own, but for I am known.
In my youth, I yearned for this title to be my identity,
But did not want to abandon my given signature.
Who is called by what I am often mistaken for?
Is there a being I am to meet that has loaned
His name to me? Is he my guardian sent by Divinity?
I have been assigned human numbers and letters.
Is this possibly the pseudonym of my spiritual form?

Sunsets on Sundays

Sunsets on Sundays; the sun fades away,
Bringing with it what bit of joy that remained.

A Lavender...

A pastel of color...
A therapeutic flower...
Assisting to be calmer...
An aid with slumber...
An oil that heals the hurt...
Ability to soothe a burn...
Abundant tales in lore...
Awe to have such power...

Caffeine / Alcohol

We all crave that poison.
We want it to flood our blood.
We drown out negative noises
With more energy or more fun.

Permanence

The lack of permanence in humanity is disheartening.
Loyalty and interest slowly dissolve as minds shift.
Thoughts and opinions as silt wash away with new waves.
Never were humans ever set in stone, and history attests;
Rather, society dictates approval, and it's ever-changing.
Legends fade and memories not erased but rewritten;
Each mind drowning in the waters we are forced to wade.
Why do recreations depend on the majority's acceptance?

Brother

We have opposing traits.
You're Type B, and I'm Type A.
We don't seem to understand each other,
Though we share that we're both stubborn.
It hurts me that we don't have a bond.
It's painful to see others' so strong.
I can't help but to feel it unfair that you
Seem to hold grudges over things we can't undo.
I do accept the faults I've caused in our past,
And I'm apologetic because of what I lack.

Juncture

Moments of bliss distract from whatever pain in my brain.
Realizing that the heaviness doesn't matter in this juncture,
But it will arise again as soon as the diversion has concluded.
Awaiting the mental torment's return is excruciating and stagnant.
Reality is on the back burner until it can no longer be delayed.
Often I am trapped between conflicting emotions—a jammed junction.
Craving the ability to command these feelings—to have them diluted.
Changes to this state cause this vessel to require a new balance.

CULTure

Everybody is free in their mind,
But what we allow to escape
Can create both friends and enemies.
It's unfair how we cannot be civil,
Independent thinkers without being
Backed by wise or attacked by blind.
No flaws allowed with no cleaning of slates.
In the age of everliving technology,
Each error, laced in unclear riddles,
Can be accessed whenever they please.
Let people be! Why should we align
With what somebody may say?
Did you consider how they feel?
Those saturated opinions are fickle.
Learn to consider things to their entirety.

Heart Hand

My heart turns into more
Than just the shape of a fist
When it needs to defend itself...

Advice to my Childhood

I wish I could go back and tell myself to enjoy things a little bit more.
If only I'd known that someday my entire perspective would distort.

His-story

I document moments of emotions
To keep a log of interesting aspects
Of life. Little records that bookmark
Frames of time to keep in mind—a lens.
Reminiscing on these notes to check
Back on memories and boxes in the dark.

Haling the Hail

Here I am again having another cold conversation in my head
All while you're likely sleeping peacefully in your warm bed.
I probably shouldn't have contacted your mother for closure,
Though she assured me she knows you, but I thought I did for sure...
Intermittent mutual points of contact often remind me of the fact
That despite my claiming, I wasn't the toxic being in the pack.
Throwing tantrums and creating your drama along with storms
Never was clear to me until seeing from afar and watching them form.
Thinking back, your blood always was as a tall drink with extra ice—
Thin and cold. You mistreated me, and as much as I want to act in spite...
Somehow I still feel residual pain, though you don't know of your power.
Were you falling for me? You caused my ninth cloud's fall—a painful shower.

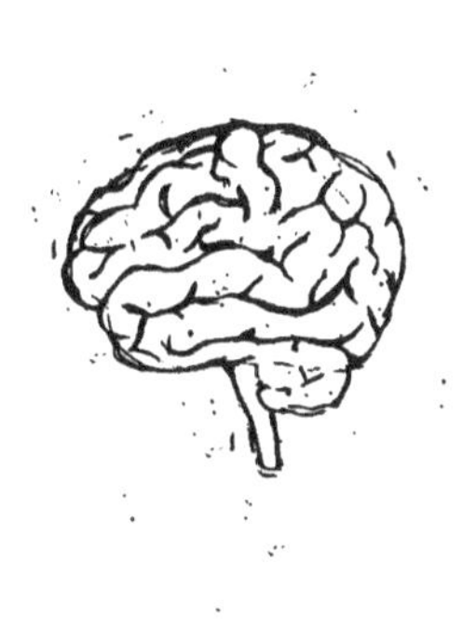

Anger

It's so comfortable yet so painful.
It's the emotion I seem to feel the most.
It feels good to let it reign over me,
But coming off of that high is torment.
After each incident, I feel like a fool.
I just crave to master more self control.
To let it out requires my justifying.
Acting on it or not is a tournament.

Sorrow

I feel so broken; my heart is vacant, and my face flat.
I want to cry to release the pressure behind my eyes,
But it's stuck at the threshold; sorrow is lurking at the rim
Without being able to find its escape from the dark wells.
There's just no justifiable means for intentional alleviation.
Because of this, any trace of emotion that I can latch to
Becomes mine, and I feel them alongside even characters.
I tear up as my sorrow proceeds to tear up my heart.

In Monochrome

They want us to be uniform–
Not straying too far from their doctrine.
They discourage freedom in forms
Of differing thoughts and opinions.
You may think you know to whom I
Am referring, but they're similarly defined.
They want everybody to match or closely coordinate.
The colors I choose clash with the agendas they actuate.

Mind/Them

What they preach
Is not truly peace.
They say to love, but force hate and lies.
They say to accept, yet they deny.
They say to be open minded
While they're already decided.

Soap Box on Soap Operas

Drama finds me, though I'm clean.
It is never what I seek.
I am framed often–
Enclosed like a coffin.
They think they know,
But they really don't.
I simply cannot escape
The situations entertained.

Mad at Myself

As much as I coach myself
To be infallible, I constantly fail.
I try not to be damaging, but
I keep breaking what's on the shelf.
Raging chaos has me derailed
Often; I can't punish myself enough.

Versus Verses

Always crosscheck when humans make a claim.
Open The Book, search the pages, and validate.
Don't be fooled by a rank or manmade title,
Trust the Words if they're truly from The Holy Bible.

New Era

It seems that after a dark age,
Everything has been renewed.
New year, new car, new phone, new job...
The unfortunate side of this is new anxieties.

O' my God

I have faith.
Still I believe what I was raised...
Maybe it's not in the same
Exact ways,
But it is Yahweh.

Chaotic Neutral

You and I are both aware that you need help...
Though I'm here for you, you once said yourself
That I need to stop trying to fix what I thought
Needed fixing. You seldom admit when you're distraught.
You always projected your own demons onto me.
They painted my character, but through your eyes only.
Intermittently, I see blips of the person whom I befriended,
But that person is often laced with supplements.
When we dispute now, I see that you argue the same.
I make attempts to change and keep the conversation tame.
As much as I want to help, you truly are toxic
To me; I won't abandon you—I want to assist, but it's chaotic.
You have yet to unlock your potential because you bind
Yourself to poison. You're loved and talented but unwise and blind.

Bowling Your Eyes

As you stand by rolling your eyes
Or judging the "weird guy" across from you,
And assuming he is an attention seeker...
Just know that he is actually pretty broken.
Outrageous behavior is a coping mechanism.
It's honestly not to make a scene or be seen.
Why can't people just let others exist?
I try not to let petty things bother me, but they do.
I don't want to allow myself to be a victim
Of something so insignificant and stupid.
I just keep telling myself and my friends
That it doesn't matter, and that I'm okay
When deep within I know that is far from the truth.

Gay (Archaic)

I'm just not afraid of myself like others.
I express myself in ways that bother.
People can't pin me, so they label me
With what makes sense to them as they deem.

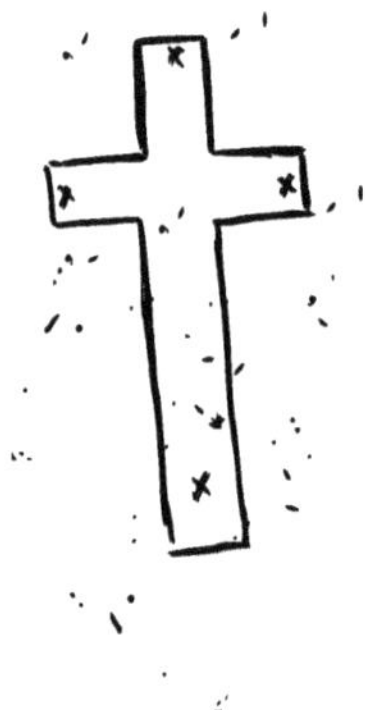

Past Tense

I keep wishing I could have lived in another era—different timing...
Then again, it's probably more interesting in my fantasy than in actuality.

Blue & Red

As much as you deserve it, it hurts me
To treat you even slightly as bad as you
Treat me... It is painful to defend myself.

Frustrated

The world around me
Is constantly evolving,
But I don't fit the norms.
Into my skin it bores.
Nobody wants to listen–
Only teach their lessons.
History cannot be altered,
Only buried and covered.
If we seek fallacies within
Anything, we will find them.
It is important to continue
In good light, but can't undo
The transgressors' sins.
If civility is lost, there's no win.
Adjust your focus and admit
That you too are a hypocrite.
We are all guilty of something,
So stop scrutinizing everything.

Blips of Bliss

It's strange that I find feelings of bliss
To be odd, uncomfortable, and suspicious.
Finding that things in recent history
That still incite joy is such a relief.

Noncompliant

People don't know how to react
When they make attacks
On my choices or personal taste,
And my response it to continue to embrace
Instead of complying to their judgment.
I don't alter my blueprints
To conform to what they think
I should or should not have in my ink.

The Guys

It's awfully dramatic of me
To well up at a picture I see.
I painted myself into many words;
All of which proved to be absurd.
I always looked to the other guys
Hoping I'd grow into them, but lies
Kept me self-conscious and insecure.
I want to use this to become inspired.

Broken Window

It's like I reincarnated into your actions in that moment
Because what I thought initially comical and innocent
Transformed into spiraling regret–total lament.
Now shards lie in relationships and things broken;
Somehow I caused reactions, but none at my own hand.

The Bridge

The mind is the bridge between the body and the soul/spirit.
The heart and the brain are often interchanged.

Angst

A whole new strain of anxiety
Recently started possessing me.
What I used to have enough control
Over is now deciding to take its toll.
I cannot exist in a crowded space–
Feeling it exaggerate what once was a trace.

In Dispair

I feel it all in my chest;
Residual effects in my head.
Afraid to seek help–helpless.
Cannot allow it to become a weapon.
Suffering through all of this agony
Because I know soon it will be subsiding.

Badnight

The night falls; eventually, the lids of my eyes do too—
Gradually, initially, then abruptly, so does my mood.
An ongoing struggle that persists even after a good day;
It's unexplainable and unstable, and for relief, I pray.

4:00 PM

As I have aged,
Moments in the day
That I used to dread
Have become the best.

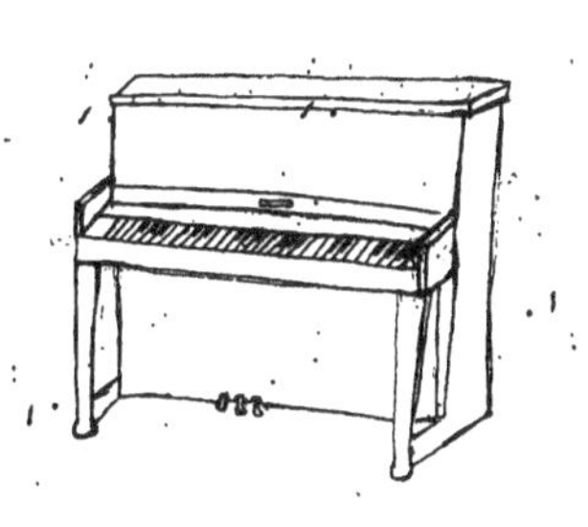

Wasps and Raindrops

I wish I could just cry, but my skin is thicker now.
I need to release the pain I've been harboring somehow.
The little stings just don't have enough poison in them
To release the floodgates and flush out the venom.

Not Knight

Remember not to fight others' battles
Unless it threatens your own castle.

Dear Stranger,

Does it feel good to belittle somebody on the internet that you don't even know? What makes it okay for you to try to force acceptance on topics that you promote, then to turn around and disrespect a random human being? It seems that you probably are just going about your day after our exchange, but now, I'm who's crying in the dark because how you treated me in a comment thread. It only added to the chaos within me. Calling me dense while you're naïve and can't comprehend the complexity of the point I was making. All I wanted to do was have a conversation. All I did was make a counter statement. You and the others like you ganged up on me and attacked without even trying to comprehend my words. Now I know to keep quiet because if I disagree with anything you preach, I will be verbally assaulted. I suggested to you to be kind, much like your kind always say to do, yet you ignored it and continued to spread your hypocritical hate.

They don't listen.

Being disrespected,
And my intelligence
Is questioned
Over a difference
In our opinions.
Feeling threatened
Are my emotions
As I am punished
For any opposition.
No active engagement.
They don't listen.

Parting and Parties

I've learned that neither liberals nor conservatives can handle when you challenge their way of thinking. They each want to blindly follow their pack because that's easier as well as more comfortable. Always question common beliefs and policies. It seems to me that they're just falling into that pattern that is tradition, just with new meaning. We the people are to blame for the great division.

Commutes

Habitual tendencies—sometimes it's important to oppose.
If you typically go fast, take it slow.
Don't just obey autopilot, take another road.
Enjoy an entirely different route home.

Jobs

Manipulation of my surroundings to fulfill my needs–
To make jobs more of an ease for me.
As I enter unfamiliar environments, I quietly
Observe until I can exploit systems efficiently.

Aries

I don't believe in the zodiac signs,
Though they do seem to often align.
A stubborn powerhouse, they describe;
Ramming through situations of hard times.
It's fun for me to pretend even if they're lies
Because I actively strive to achieve what's wise.

Stoic

Being hidden is useful for my pride's sake,
But nobody will ever know of my masked pain
Unless I draw back those layers and let them.
Sometimes the thick skin I grew is like a prison.
I want to relinquish these emotions, but I cannot.
Needing support, but wanting to keep them blocked.

Normalcy

You expected me to congratulate you
In that moment that you told me your news.
I apologize for my lacking reaction, but I
Only feel saddened when I hear of milestones in life.
I don't mean to be selfish, and I don't expect
You to understand–typical behaviors, I naturally reject.

of Fire

Supposedly my natural element;
It makes sense due to its eternal conflict.
Warmth and life or pain and death?
Destruction and hell or energy and light?
I don't claim it for my spirituality, but my head
Hosts endless wars with swaying fights.
Easily ignited and difficult to control–
Just as my emotions and unlike my soul.
Passion burns in my heart but leaves eschar.
Ashes whirl around my skull like a snow globe.
They are the remains from battles and scars.
As I die down, the embers of myself are still aglow.

Kids

I never really liked children—not even as a child.
I am sick of people saying, "You'll understand someday."
Stop placing me into generalizations and traditions.
I'm not closing the door to the possibilities, however,
I currently don't wish to partake in that lifestyle.
It's never been my desire, but maybe that will change.
I get glimpses of understanding, but it's not my mission.
I don't want to forfeit the opportunity, but it's a decision forever.

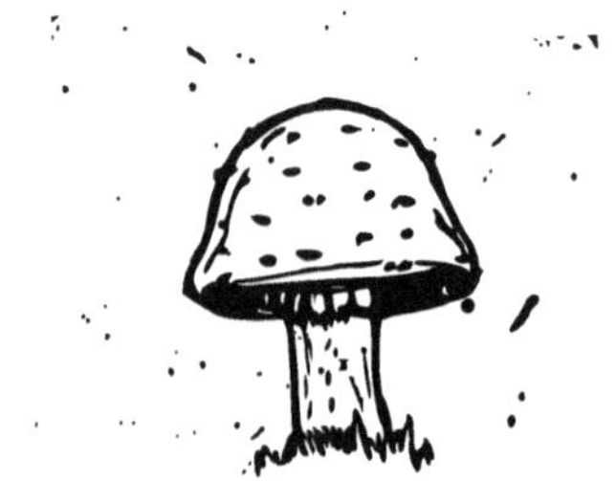

Pseudo-sleep

Not ready to be bothered or seen.
I'm in a state of faking my sleep.
Quietly taking in all of my surroundings;
I'm not engaging, but I'm listening.

ADHD

Undiagnosed and self-diagnosed–
Random outbursts of suppressed energy.
Difficulty focusing on even my entertainment;
My thoughts and processing are speed-runners.
Unaware people often assume I'm dense or slow,
But I am many steps ahead, typically.
It's constant trials yet a superpower, not mindlessness.
Can zone into absence, then able to hyper-focus greater.

Depressive Phases

A never-ending cycle in my life
Consists of these depressive phases.
I fear for their return as my blight
Because I know the relief is temporary.
Just as the night, darkness surrounds light;
My mentation constantly wanes and waxes.
It's scary to me when I become merry
Because I know it'll soon lapse and decline.

Food

Though I'm not morbidly obese,
I recognize that I have an addiction.
My mood shifts if I cannot eat
Whatever my cravings' suggestion.
It's challenging to control the urge
To absentmindedly consume
And indulge with the moment's spur.
Emotional or bored–the answer's not food.

Subconscious

I feel only but a trace–
An essence of negativity.
Inhabiting those moments
Is something I can't pinpoint.
I feel increasingly displaced
While held in its captivity.
Collecting no atonement
For nonconsensual joint.

Spiraling

I can keep emotions reserved when it's outward,
But I'm so vulnerable, candid, and honest to art.
I don't mean to be so standoffish, but
I just don't know how to process love
Amongst other feelings. I continue to circle
Back around to confusion that's nonverbal.

Social Loner

I want to just leave everything I know behind.
I never can fulfill what I emotionally crave.
I want to abandon everybody, but then I'll
Miss them all whenever I actually escape.
Reuniting is equally as challenging as leaving.
I always feel awkward and lost regardless.
My thoughts and feelings keep presenting
In codes and languages that I cannot process.

Hold Me / Don't Touch Me

I want to feel cared about,
But I want to be left alone.
When I feel, it's laced with doubt.
My thoughts simultaneously oppose.

Slaughter Not in Vain

I do not believe in killing animals without purpose;
Even as small as a bug, let it continue to exist
Unless its remains will be utilized and recycled.
I despise that animals may suffer for the benefit of humans–
I am not vegan or vegetarian, but unfortunately the chain
Will continue to be vicious regardless of humanity.
Responsibly and respectfully rule with dominion and power.

Privilege?

The fact that you're able to complain about your situation
And keep your life speaks volumes of the level of your own privilege.
If you were truly oppressed, you would exhibit hesitation,
Not condemnation and cancellation with your lack of respect.

Tiring

I'm tired of sleeping.
I'm tired of eating.
I'm tired of urinating.
I'm tired of defecating.
I'm tired of working.
I'm tired of hurting.
I'm tired of breathing.
I'm tired of living.

Rhinestones

People like you bedazzle the untruths,
Making them shinier and concealing abuse.
Just because you think that it is magic
Doesn't negate the fact that it's still plastic.
I don't want a pretty apology or story,
I want facts of the matter even if they're ugly.
They may make it look nice on the exterior,
But upon closer inspection, its value is inferior.

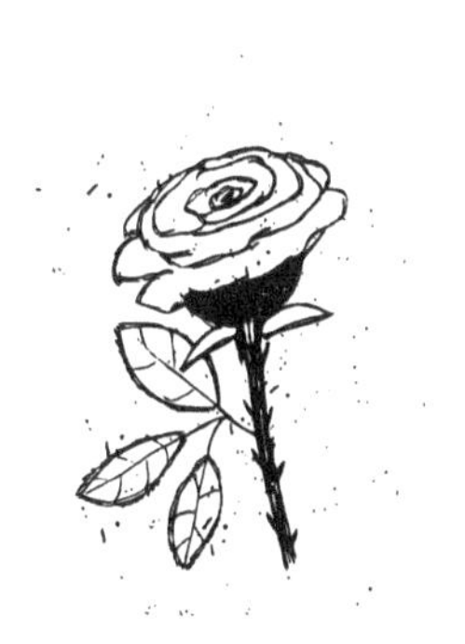

Anxiety About Anxiety

I can't easily do anything.
People often think I'm boring.
Held back by my own fears
That persist through the years.
I'm afraid to attempt new things
That are considered normal.
I'm terrified of side-effects of anxiety.
I don't want to panic and lose control.

Antisocial Media

If you truly want to be informed, disconnect from the media which is deformed. We are all puppets in their algorithms' mapping. Do we ever actually know what is happening? Do we actually know the facts? We only know what we are directed to. All we see is a dramatic story threaded together by currencies–fabrication woven into our minds and sewn into our eyes. We are all being played. We are pawns in a money game. Your sharing of that information isn't education, it's manipulation possessed by your unaware hands meeting the magnate's demands.

Report

I was standing in support,
Then y'all went overboard.
Now I revoke my rapport.

My Chaos

Not going to lie,
But tonight
I want to die.
So much conflict
In my mind.
It's so chaotic,
I could cry.

Serial Backstabber

I run around
To try to pull out
All the knives you stabbed
In everybody's backs.

Burned at the Steak

I don't understand why people act like people should be burned at the stake
Over opinions and preferences on how to properly cook and consume steak.

Unsettling and Unsafe

It is unsettling how we are never completely safe.
Anybody can become a fallen victim at any stage.

Shadows and Spirits

Off in the distance, I see movement.
It caught my eye within that moment,
But where did it wander off and vanish?
I'll never know if it was a shadow or spirit.

Sad/Mad

Typically when people are exhibiting a saddened reaction,
I am observing the topic from another angle with anger.

Untruths

People don't want to listen to the truth.
They don't want to be corrected on the untruths
That their deaf, gossiping tongues spew.
Their own mouths gabbing is all they want to listen to.

The Game of...

I did not request to exist,
So why I have to participate?
I despise the processes of life.

Later Pain

I know that I am not enduring all my future pain,
And I try not to dread what may be next;
It is hard, however, to imagine having to sustain
Similar ailments and trials again, if not worse.

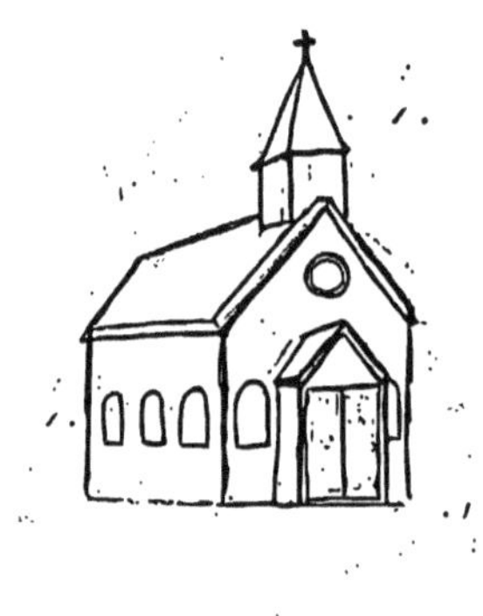

The Palette of Privilege

It's not a matter of opinion, it's a matter of personal experience.
Undoubtedly, every skin color has its own perks and privilege.
Neither side of the argument will agree with this viewpoint,
But that's the problem: people only look from their standpoint.

Bodies

I'm often disgusted by my body staring back at me from the mirrored room,
And I'm not afraid to admit that we males have bodies too.

Force Field / Forced Feel

Though anxiety has likely decreased my life expectancy,
It has also served as a protection—much like a force field.
The fears—irrational and rational—inhabiting the background of my mind
Prevent me from making irreversible decisions in the foreground of my life.

Circular Pondering

So many theories with no true means to explain.
To choose one over another requires just as much faith.
I choose Jesus because of my personal experience,
Though I do wonder how did He come to be?
Why did He design everything to operate like this?
Why do things not make any sense to me?
That's where I have to stop thinking before confusion
Takes over my thoughts in the form of depression.

Medical Attention

Why do I feel the need to add pain to an injury?
Persistent pain is frustrating and eventually leads
To me lashing out, attempting to attack the hurt in me.

Consistency of Consistency

To most, consistency is as a thin sauce
Spread overtop of problems but not strong
Enough to mask the bitterness or compliment the flavor.
Selfishness needs to stop being the focus for favors.
Be more consistent and less watered down.
Don't thin out in the heat and integrity is found.
Be attentive to the inescapable hypocrisy
That is welled within each of us deeply.
Have openness to learning with steadfast roots–
A backbone with willingness to respectfully debate, too.

Thread

I feel like I am dangling in the polluted air by a thread.
I thought I was wearing a coat of many colors,
But now I question if it was tailored for me or if I just put it on.
I felt so secure before, but have I outgrown this? I dread.
I have accepted that I cannot comprehend it like the others,
And I have realized it is just as simple to doff it as it is to don.
"You reap whatever you sew" so I thought–it is what they said;
However, sometimes you must still tread murky water.
It does not mean you cannot wash and dry your clothes on a new dawn.

Forgot my...

I got out of my car, and I forgot my crutch.
Something I don't need, yet "need" too much.
Lights blinding my face and distracting my eyes
Create such a space from the reality drenched with lies.

God, forgive me...

God, please forgive me for I **do** know what I do.
I take full accountability with no valid excuse.
I am numb to the sins that dance upon the Earth,
But with Your Divine lens, I feel guilt through rebirth.

Saved

This is how to be saved by grace,
And through faith in His holy name.
Repent and believe on Him... It is
Not enough to acknowledge His existence...

Tech Tots

We, the children, need to be taught
So the wires in our heads can be taut.

Elitists

Why do we allow the wealthy governments to be our masters?
We have them far surpassed and beaten in numbers.
They either never knew or are too far removed,
Yet they make the decisions that we suffer through.

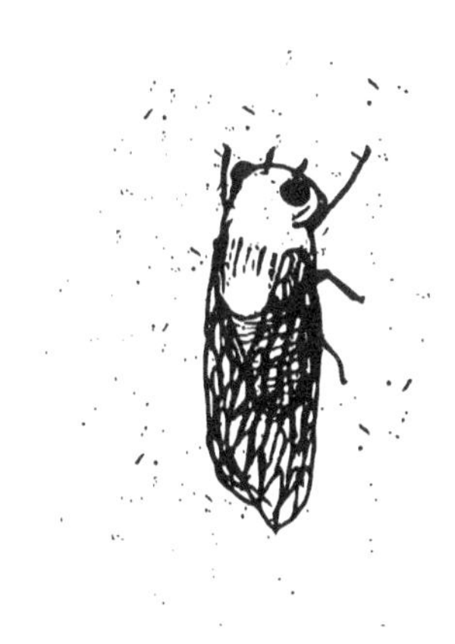

Intermittent Ideations

I always come back through this cycle.
It's a matter of ignoring the daily pain.
I often feel trapped in a labyrinth of emotions
That has no visible exit, only familiar walls.
As much as I understand the concept...
Following through with it settles differently.

Offset Me

I hate how fragile I can be.
I'd like to think I'm strong,
But if somebody says just the wrong
Thing, it'll break me so badly.

the Birds

Land masses, water bodies, and skies—
Exploring their perimeters
With unique abilities and grace.

Zillennial

I fall on a very fine line between two generations.
I can/can't relate with either side of my surrounding peers.
I don't like being categorized into/by either side.
I renders me in a state of confusion with an identity crisis.

Freedom of Mind

I am free to think and believe whatever I want.
If that does not align with your desires and convictions,
That simply is not a concern of mine.

Shades

I consistently have to remind myself to hold my own opinion
Without shifting it solely based on others' perspective.
Take what they say with a grain, but don't live by it
Until you have lived it and seen if with your own lens.

Heart & Cold

I don't know how to process my emotions.
I know it often comes across as cold and heartless.

Me, Myself, and God

My business and decisions are between myself and God.
They are not between me, you, and God.
My convictions are my own,
Not something you own.

Onion Tears & Opinions

Things you say to others have an impact on their mind,
And this does change it whether or not you realize.
People will fake their emotions to match yours
Until that slowly alters their own mental force.

Lapsing

When I find cures for my ailments and conditions,
I wonder how long they will last before lapsing.

1995-2005_CCM

Looking back on that era—it was so pure...
Though, I now know it probably was not,
I just did not have the ability to see the corrosion.
I long for the naïve perspective that I outgrew.

Nevermore...

She said to him, "I'll see you in the morning."
He, however, did not awaken to witness her mourning.

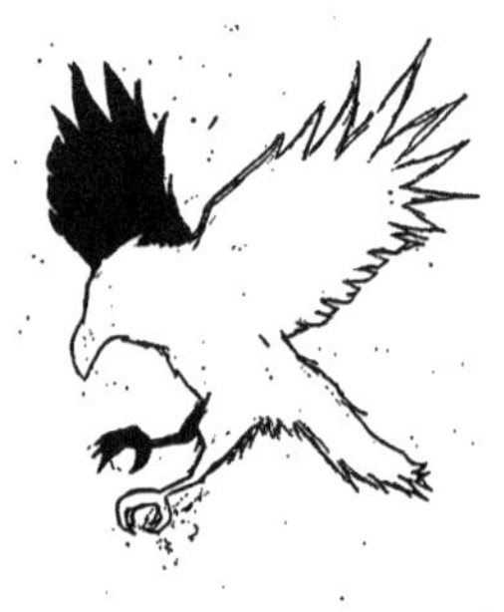

Microbullied

All my life, even now, people have made subtle jabs at my existence.
As I unravel, I am discovering the many damaged fragments
That have been buried beneath layers of my flesh over time.
After every instance, I shed thin skin to regenerate hardened callouses.
From my taste to my voice and even genetic, physical appearance—
I can't even determine if it's bottled, but I don't generally whine.
I've heard it all, and it has truly placed my mentality off-balance.
Intermittently, it will occur to me that I've been damaged by what they said.

Lessons of Depression

I've learned that I have to keep myself excited to ward off depression. Though that isn't always attainable, that seems to be the lesson.

Opinionated

I'm learning that voicing unasked for opinions isn't being strong.
It's just seeking drama and arguments that occupy my time wrong.

Masking Tape

Is it worth your own misery?
Is reappropriating issues really protecting?
It's ironic that half of humanity
Is preaching humaneness while dehumanizing.
What good is saving lives
That now only want to die?

Præy

Just pray **for** them–
Don't prey **on** them.

Progressions

Your good news is actually devastating to me.
My excitement for you is only my pretending.
I don't want to come across lackluster or rude,
But I don't want to be inauthentic and untrue.
I'm sorry I can't be that friend that you want/need;
I'm just as disappointed that I can't for you.

Faith Based Practice

Everything we do in existence operates by the means of faith. To claim that faith is fiction is asinine. Whether it be spiritually or physically, faith is the thread that inherently binds our mentality.

Excruciating

It's excruciating to sit here desiring to elicit a change,
But being unable to find the motivation to put it in motion.

Genes & 3 Wishes

I wish I could get excited like that...
I wish I could exhibit normal behaviors...
I wish I could be that vulnerable...
However, part of me loves how abnormal I am.

Ahead of a Head

It's a double edged sword to withhold thought processes,
But I don't want to alter theirs... I prefer them genuine.
I probably wouldn't be considered stupid if I initially explained,
But simultaneously, I'd rather catch them off guard with my wit
Rather than have to work harder to overcome their schemes.

Proud to Be Ashamed

Somebody tell me how I am supposed to exist
When I am ashamed of everything I'm proud of...?

Is it me or them?

I've spent so much time feeling innocent,
But maybe it really is me that is the problem?
Unless I'm just outnumbered by them?

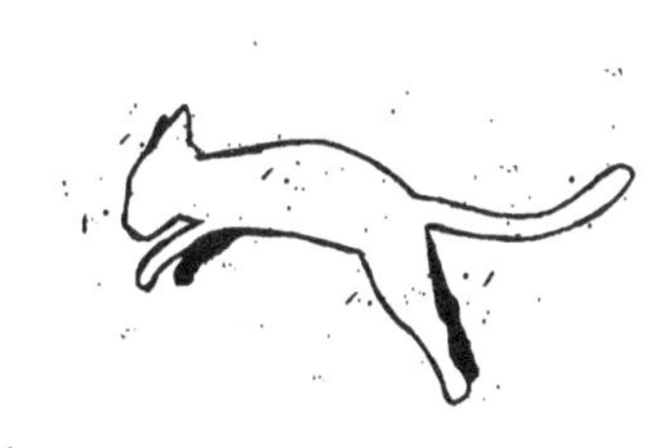

Old News, New Noose

I'm learning that what the old-fashioned news preaches is generally bent truth or opposite.

While others are living by it, I'm becoming wiser because I am not paying it any attention.

Why is it that reporters report on subjects they have no expertise on, and people believe it?

The Late Years

Wanting to
reminisce, yet to
avoid any sense of
nostalgia because it's
too painful to yearn
for the late years...

Whelmed

This concept isn't out of my ordinary,
But it's harder for me to do anything
That anybody else could do so easily–
That's the negative power of anxiety.
Practically anything you can imagine,
I'm probably stressed about paired with urgency.
My imagination is relentlessly overactive–
Working overtime but abundant in creativity.

Repression of Escaping Depression

Why is it so comfortable to stay in a depressive state?
Oftentimes, I will see a temporary exit, but I evade
Simply because of the small percentage of self pity.
Particles of pride are not worth the pain emitting.

Wool

You follow a pattern,
Meanwhile, I'm a designer.

Intonation & Intention

Just because you iterate "please" and "thanks"
Does not allow exemption from intended hate.
Just because you are being honest from your head
Does not mean that it is something that should be said.

Crazy, Caregiving, Controlling

How you act isn't showing that you're caring...
It's simply poor regulation of your emotions
At the expense of everybody in your vicinity.

Removing Myself

I constantly feel like I am the problem in the crowd.
Lately, I avoid because I assume it is better without me around.

Δ's

I'm terrified of the internal changes that I subconsciously undergo.
Is it justified? I generally circle back to previous phases, though.
I constantly am sifting through life and attempting to make sense
Of my thoughts and emotions. I do know I'm not lukewarm nor on the fence.

Running from You > Running into You

Why can't I just march into the store when I see your car?
Or even when I see you ambulating another aisle?
You're at fault, not me—you lied with your despicable tongue.
My heart rate shouldn't increase when I see your face.
You wronged me, yet you nominate yourself as the victim.
I cut the ties that you thought were chains because of your mentality.
You thought you were untouchable and omni-powerful.
I'm not somebody you can buy nor impress with tangible gifts.
If only you'd move your residency to some distant land
Because I shouldn't be punished for your wicked ways.

Suppressed Spirit

I've learned to start acknowledging the issues I feel with my spirituality.
God is well-aware of how I'm feeling and what I'm thinking,
So why am I trying to hide and suppress the truth that lives within?
It's between myself and God, and it helps me with healing and acceptance.

Monophonic Stereotypes

I am completely for equality with disdain for generalization,
However, I am capable of admitting that stereotypes exist for a reason.

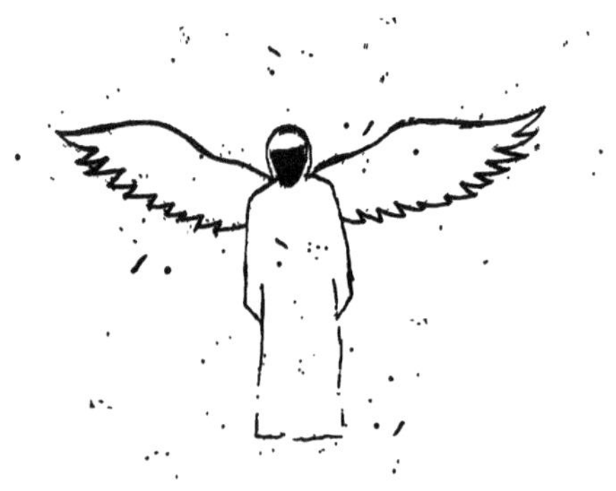

Organs and Instruments

How can you believe in divinity,
But not believe in mental disease?
A brain is just as much of an organ
As an organ is an instrument.
Instruments need tune-ups,
And brains need checkups.
Whether those tools are physical,
Or in other instances metaphorical,
They can be used to assist
With whatever the diagnosis...

Be Kind

It's easy to assume and prioritize outrage,
But I urge you to view from another page.
We never know what lurks behind somebody's face.
Reactions flippantly, absentmindedly escape
From throats before realization of their pain.
After chaotic verbiage is expelled, it's too late.
Take the time to be kind and redirect the hate.

Attention Seeking

Even if somebody is lying and seeking attention,
Would it really ail you to provide it for them?
Depending on situation and circumstance,
Maybe all they need is that caring chance.

Young Adults

The world we live in now is hyperactive.
Generations apply the rules from their time
To the current age, then consider us stupid
For the impossibility to abide by them and comply.

Too New

I thought that a complete remodeling of my life
Would be completely positive and beneficial.
It's not that it wasn't, it's that I didn't consider
The possibility of it being this overwhelming.

Singing into the Ocean

There's such power and satisfaction in singing into the ocean.
As each wave crashes, it paints the stories of the sea.
The tides talk while the wind whispers the secrets of the motions.
Between each melody, I breathe in air that is warm and salty.
If only I could bottle up the sound's waves and use it like a potion.
It would result in immense healing and a more accessible remedy.

Identify Identity

I may appear as something easily identifiable,
But there are far more layers than your scope can discern.
Though what you see on my surface is genuine,
It's also abundant enough to utilize as a form of defense.
To live authentically has always been uncomfortable.
Inaccurate attributes are attached along with assigned worth
Which can feel suffocating and send emotions into descent.
I often remind myself to choose when I activate my offense.

HAILEY's Comet

You made the executive decision to excommunicate me.
For years, I was distraught how easily I was disposed of.
Your hands were washed of me, but mine were catching
The tears that I cried that you didn't care that you brought.
To think that I held you so high–you were among the few
That I would entrust with my life... What a lie that I painted
Unknowingly, however, you actually did save me from you.
At the expense of another, my witnessing disclosed that you're tainted.
I never noticed how toxic you were from such close proximity,
But now it's obvious to me that you practiced the role of the victim.
Seeing your attitude's perimeters put your mother's traits on display.
Maybe it's because you are cursed from your spoiled entitlement.

Feng Shui

It is vital to the mind to maintain the balance.
Physical organization leads to mental order.
I have suspicion that there is a spiritual aspect
That entwines with all surrounding inanimate matter.

Fearing Peers While Peering Years

I dread that my comfort, convenience, and satisfaction
Often depend on societal demand, actions, and reactions.
I crave to control my surroundings including what affects me,
But that in itself would be extremely overwhelming.

PDA PTSD

It's not that I'm embarrassed of you,
It's that I'm ashamed of what I'll do.

Double Edged Nerves

Anxiety prevents me from making poor decisions,
However, it also prevents me from making wise ones.

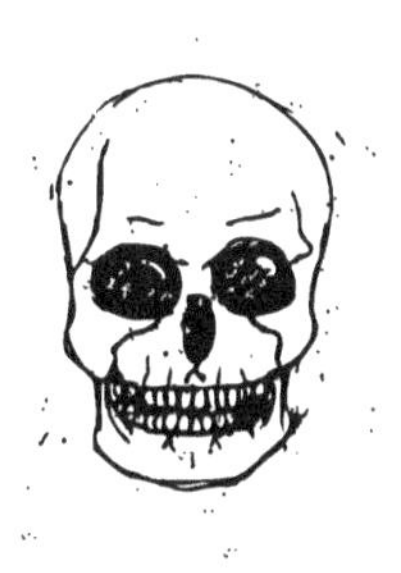

Insecurity Breach

Confidence is key, but I'm no locksmith.
No break in or entry through walls I deal with;
My flesh doesn't feel like a safe for my guts–
I feel exposed to everybody, especially those I distrust.
There are moments of positive morale, but
It's usually met with or succeeded by my contempt.

Silver Linings

I believe everything happens for different reasonings,
And that there can be silver linings with anything.
Tragedy can result in positive outcomes
Just as prosperity can lead to the glum.

Comedy

They say laughter can be the most effective remedy
That can combat tragedy when utilized appropriately.
I wholeheartedly agree with this theory as it is a necessity.
Though sometimes, it is used offensively, and other times, defensively.

Hypocrites

I can be a hypocrite—
I will definitely admit.
Who is not as such?
Everybody is, to be blunt.
I truly do despise it,
But all possess that sin.
What makes the difference is that
Some attempt to avoid those acts.

i am sick

I am sick in my head.
It is more than a head cold.
The sin craves to be fed.
As it indulges, it poisons my soul.
Stealing sleep away from my bed,
My emotional state grows old.

Balance & Beliefs

You utilize an outdated method of thinking. I understand being steadfast in your beliefs, however, claiming to be truth-seeking while blatantly disregarding the truth presented before you is outright ignorant and obstinate. Recycling arguments that are inapplicable is not proving your case—it is failing your system. It is crucial to have a balance between understanding the opposing logic to more accurately and efficiently present your belief system. You should not allow your emotions to dictate your thoughts, beliefs, or opinions. They may serve as a guideline, but logic should sketch the blueprints. Separate your feelings from reality.

About Christianity

If I am incorrect, I lose nothing while gaining the folly.
If I am correct, I gain everything while losing the faulty.

Worked Up Over Overworking

I'm a hard worker, but I'm not going to work harder
Unless I see it as beneficial for me or the need of others.
Corporations view employees as expendable and replaceable.
I've witnessed parents fooled to feed their family–turn those tables.
The cataracts of the work force and heritage blind previous generations.
Work smarter and ignore certain traditions while seeking better solutions.
Society demands far too much from everybody while people feel trapped.
There's a healthy balance to maintain that extremes cannot seem to track.
Somewhere in between being a decent, reliable human being
And being present for your family–living not simply existing.
I refuse to be a puppet to this machine of revenue and greed.
My hands and my mind are my own–I have my boundaries.

Seasonal Shift

I crave that feeling of immense jubilation that each seasonal shift brings.
I do not have a favorite season as they each have a marvelous quality.
From the vibrant array of colors and blooming vegetation that is spring.
To the brightness, warmth, and life in the air that summer breathes.
From the autumn canvases displaying beginnings of rebirth and the beauty of falling
To the chill of winter that revitalizes systems and encourages inner warmth emphasizing.

Neon Pastel

We exist within colors contrasting.
Harsh vibrancy meets soft subtlety–
Deciphering opposition and embracing
The differences while living and loving.
Differing tastes in art or disliking something
Is not law but simply your opinion and thinking.
The attraction of opposites is a valid factor.
All variables in a spectrum can contribute to chapters.

Elders

The late cornerstones who framed all that we know.
To experience their stories—the tragedy and the glory.
I feel so honored to grow from them, and claim them as my own.
The blatant disrespecting will not be tolerated from me.
I am so grateful for those who sacrificed so we could reap what they sewed.
Eternal love to the elderly that I had the privilege to bond with or simply meet

Loyal

Loyalty is not turning your nose up or your back to somebody you claim.
Our relationship is sacred to me—a holy cloth never to be stained.
Years will persist along with hardships, but my love will not be in vain.
A season may bring forth a drought, even so, I will still defend your name.
Life is already so feeble, so I strive to reinforce my people with invincible frames.

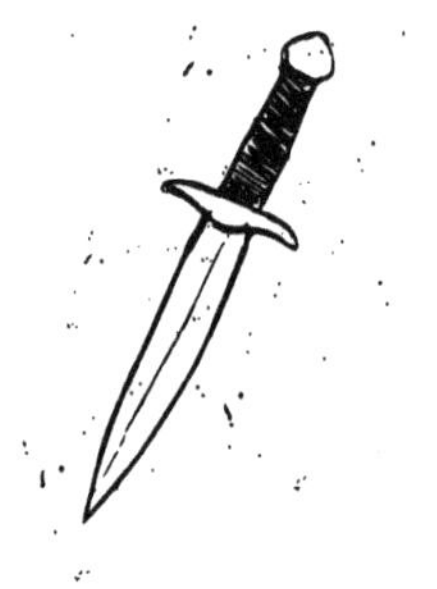

Bags

Being resourceful–utilizing surroundings...
Collecting fragments and continuously learning...
Adapting and gaining new gear to store in bags...
Taking on new tools from the nearby comrades...
Trying times while attempting to stay prepared...
Having gadgets on hand assisting others' prayers...

Paranoia

Sometimes I think back at success and fear for what could've been a failure.
Why can't I just enjoy life's offerings without the panic driving its fangs in?
Vehicles that pass me by–I often tense up at the thought of getting shot.
I hide in my own front yard as neighbors walk by in fear of inconsequential judgment.
Obsessively locking doors just in case a psychopath decides to socialize.
I am constantly on watch duty with my guard shielding us as we navigate the public.
I won't claim that my behavior isn't odd, but the evils in the world are to blame.

Considerate

Consideration is a tragically lost art.
People are inherently self-centered,
But we all should attempt to role play.
Try to feel how your actions will mark
Whomever it is that you will encounter,
But be mindful not to harm yourself along the way.

Sleep Procrastination

As I waste my day with empty distractions,
Revenge will set in with sleep procrastination.
I desire to revamp my sleep schedule,
However, I prioritize leisure over productive or restful.
A night owl with ADHD describes me to a T...
Somehow sleepiness and tranquillity motivates me.

~~Follow~~ Your Heart **Is Deceitful**

Such a lie is encouraged and painted all over art.
The heart is deceitful, and emotions are fleeting.
A symbiotic relationship between two organs is important.
I advise to think with your brain and feel with your heart.
Logic is for wise decisions while feelings promote empathy.
The issue is that they are too often divided by the divisive.

Subtle Anger

Maybe I am just bitter.
I cannot relinquish that subtle anger.
I suppose I am the issue,
But how am I supposed to continue?

Unbothered

I can't get any rest.
Demons try to arrest.
All these calamities
Followed by catastrophes.
They smell my blood
From my contusions.
Every single minute cut
Is painfully adding up.
They are constantly breaking
Vehicles that can take me.
As soon as something's fixed
Another thing is breakin'.
I'll prevail over any obstacle.
I'll modify and adapt to be the pinnacle.
I will turn anything into a tool.
I'm learning to shed my inner fool.
I am a resourceful problem-solver.
I will strive to be unbothered.

Empathy for the Dead

With every death I encounter,
My heart gains another fracture.
It breaks me to bear witness
To a body that lay there lifeless.
I often wonder how fate could have spared
As I imagine and relate with those who cared.

Be careful what you say to me because I'll remember it.

I will forgive, but I won't forget.
I don't hate you, but it shifts my perspective.
I won't be vindictive or hold a grudge,
I now know, however, what you're capable of.

Friends That Are Family

Here's to the people whom I've encountered
Through unexpected circumstances and events
That I'm so humbled and honored to consider
As some of my very best, dear friends.

Speak ON

It's not that it's simply complaints.
If nobody speaks on it, it won't change.

Inferiority

Sometimes I can't help but to feel inferior
Though I'm aware that in some aspects I'm superior.
We all have talents and skills that are innate,
But oftentimes I simply want to evaporate.
In my mind, my confidence is a force to be reckoned with,
However, when the reality of these situations sets in,
It reconfigures my mood, thoughts, and opinions of myself.
Anxiety violates me as I shut down whilst I feel so useless.

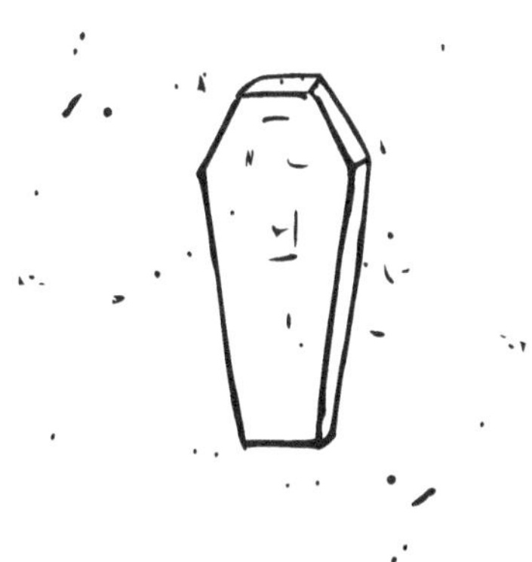

Delivery Matters

The problem isn't always the message,
Sometimes it's simply your delivery method.

Thunderstruck

I once heard a woman say that she loved the sound of thunder... She thought it was beautiful. In that moment, I remembered how important it is to view commonly misunderstood events in a positive light.

Ask Questions

Don't just settle for information you're presented. It baffles me that nobody challenges the pressures of the directors—they just conform to the demands. This is why nothing changes. This is why things get worse. We need to band together in great numbers, but we will never happen. Things won't change because I'm one person. I've always been one person.

Love Letters & Suicide Notes

In those moments of overwhelming grief, it is easy to bypass the love we are gifted as well as the love we have to give. Life seems to be confusion laced with intermittent feelings that we either choose to embrace or that overtake our thoughts. At times, those emotions are appropriately distributed, however at other times, they are not. The ever-changing waves in our minds cause us to chase the rushes of jubilation that dopamine and serotonin elicit. To say that sorrow is invalid only brings an increased level of grief to the forefront. It is difficult to exist in such a cruel, cutthroat world, but we have no viable option otherwise. People can be so vicious yet so charitable. Sin bores its vile vessels, equipped with serrated claws, into any avenue it can locate. This creates chaos more violent than anything imaginable, yet it inhabits this dimension so silently. Brokenness and vulnerability can be beautiful, but at the cost of enduring immense heartache. Craving death seems just as sensible as seeking love in those moments of agony. Ideations often creep in and become so tempting, but fear keeps it at bay until those feelings subside. These complex emotions continue to bleed onto papers until the misery deceases. When it is impossible to decipher a love letter from a suicide note is when it will be apparent that what we know cannot be revived.

Destructive Behavior

I feel so confused and desolate.
Pleading for redemption with no answer
While feeling so ignored each time
Are the things that keep me obstinate.
I know it is wrong, but I want to feel danger.
There must be unknown reasons and rhymes.
Sitting in silent faith harboring grief and ache
Create such a wave of devastation and anger.
I then reminisce somebody so sublime
Who would be disappointed in this pain.
It makes me reconsider desires of destructive behavior,
Though I will never comprehend or accept this goodbye.

Grief Insomnia

As another absence claims somebody's flesh,
Heaviness promptly infects my heart.
Denial and disbelief control my head
To turn dreams to nightmares in my bed.
Neon darkness that prescribes such hurt
Keeps me from peace—it's sleep I dread.

Abandøned & Bløcked

You abandoned me in a desolate space.
A mystery that only you could relinquish,
But you chose excommunication without a trace.
Now I am lost in confusion, and my skull is a prison.

Disposable

Why am I so disposable to others?
I put so much energy into my loyalty
Only to be blocked and ultimately hurt.
Wracking my brain and searching for words—
Maybe my personality simply smothers
Or maybe it's a mistake or misunderstanding.

My Fault / Default

My mind, I cannot process.
I am secretly so broken,
And nobody even knows it.
I must keep it all hidden.
With anything that happens,
I blame myself as the default
Even if it is not actually my fault.

Grieveyard Shift

In the night while everybody is sleeping,
I am left in the dark alone grieving.
God is omnipresent–unexplainable comfort He provides,
But I cannot help but to obey my sorrow's pride.
While others are in their sleep at peace,
That's when my grief sinks in its jagged teeth.

Nothing Is Real

I awaken, but am I alive?
I sleep, but when will I die?
Turning on each screen,
I soon realize that what I've seen
Could have been altered
While my cognition falters.
Interrogating myself and my sanity
Whilst questioning the digital humanity.
Is all we know of reality actually staged?
Is there a point in knowledge and faith?
As years collect on my age—while integrating—
I realize I know nothing and nobody.
I feel as though I care too much
In comparison, yet do not know how to love.

Diagonal Diagnoses

It's not **who** I am;
It's just **how** I am.

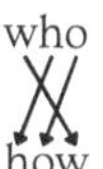

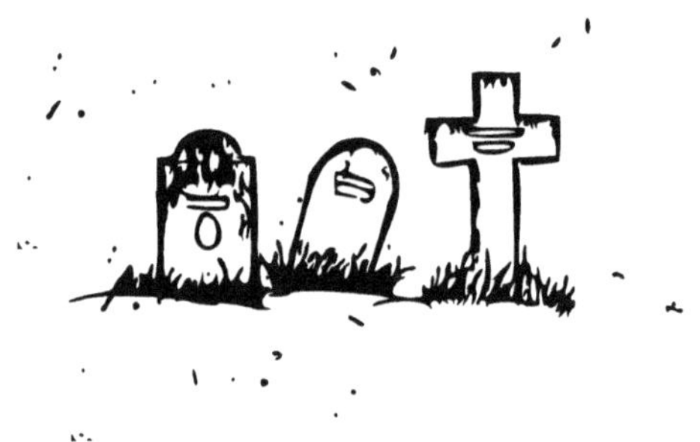

Grieving Grace's Grave

I am so sorry that I could not hold you as tightly
As I wanted to–my arms were too weak from the grief.

Me, Myself, & Eyes

I always feel like somebody is watching me—
Whether it's government, demons, or divinity.

Pretend I'm Dead

Pretend I'm dead, then tell me how you really feel about me.

Jacked

My cup runs over with each drop falling out of my eyes.
Saline streams flow down my face as I
Attempt to process these complex emotions.
I loathe death, but I have learned to respect it.
Now I drive past places we once borrowed the same ground,
And it summons memories and plans that fate did not allow.

Lovelessness

I have grown less empathetic as it seems.
Truth be told, I am not sure what I feel anymore.
Unfortunately, I have yet to master the art of love.
It is easier to project my heart towards your pain.
I cannot help but feel pathetic when it affects me.
I do not wish misery, I just want to feel something more.
This is not by choice, it is just the method of a sick brain.

Opinions of Modern Chaos

The internet is useful but evil.
Social media is a tumor of the world wide web.
I believe it is one of the worst things ever invented.
Despite all the pros, there are far greater cons.
Think about that.

Reflecting on my Reflection

Sometimes, I walk past a mirror and catch a glance of a stranger.
A face that sparks a dissociative moment within my psyche.
A chain reaction of pondering trails between my body and my mind.
If only I could be somebody else, yet I still continue to linger.
Oftentimes, I am lost in the echoes of my own negative thinking.
If only I could clean the glass and rewrite how I am defined.

Dichoto(me)

I feel like I am in an eternal, internal war.
My mind is a great divide; I am always torn.
I am decisive but the details are divisive.
In the interest of fairness, I am incisive.

Child<>Adolescent<>Adult

I forget how much things constantly evolve around me.
As much as I want to remain, things will still change.
I feel trapped in the suspension of my own confusion.

The Algorithm in the Simulation

Do we truly have any singular experiences?
Do we all share this life?
Does uniqueness even actually exist?

NPC

Sometimes, I feel like I am the main character,
And other times, I wish I was anything but that.
Life would be easier if I was mindlessly scripted.
I could fulfill my role without being a critical thinker.
I would not ever have to feel sad, mad, or bad.
Then I wonder if would even be worth it to exist?

Things & Bodies

Expect nothing.
Prepare for anything.
Be attentive to everything.
Contribute something.
Disrespect nobody.
Be kind to anybody.
Do not trust everybody.
Be somebody.

zachx.com

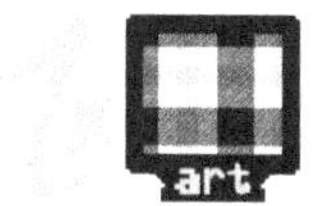

Other works by Zachx:

Chartreuse and Teal

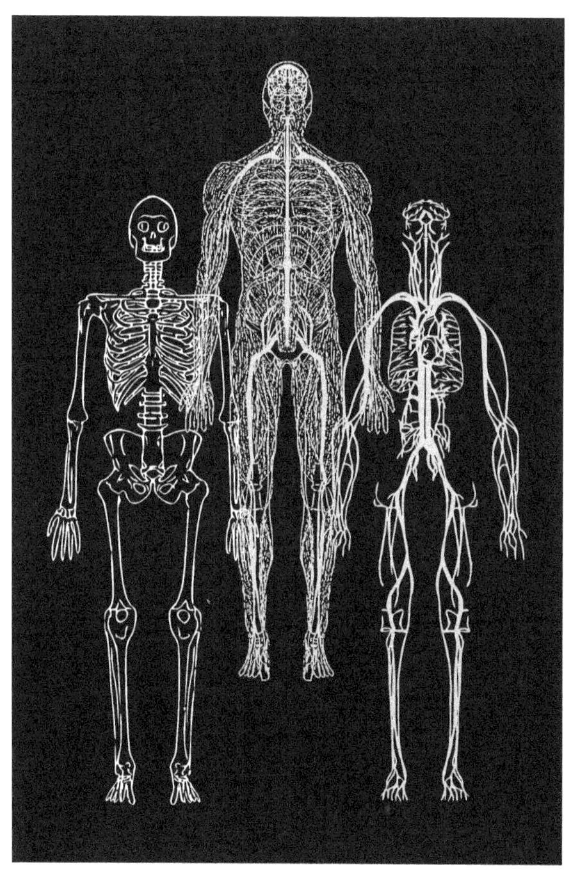

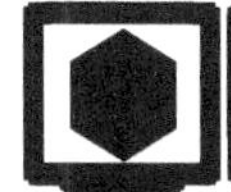 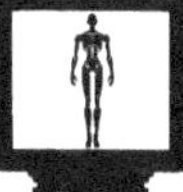 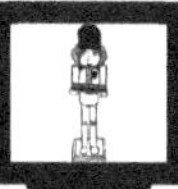    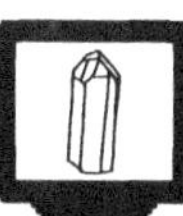 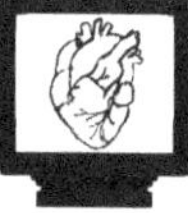

www.ingramcontent.com/pod-product-compliance
Lightning Source LLC
LaVergne TN
LVHW010613100826
845148LV00014B/2952